THE MOUTH OF HOME

To Elizabeth
On spirit,
Janell

POEMS

JANELL MOON

ARCTOS PRESS
Sausalito, California

HoBear Publications

ARCTOS ❧ PRESS
P.O. Box 401
Sausalito, CA 94966-401
CB Follett, Editor/Publisher

Copyright © 1999 by Janell Moon

Cover Art: *The Mouth of Home* by Claire Wolf Krantz
Back Cover Photograph: Bonnie Marzlak
Book Design & Typography: Christi Payne, Book Arts

Library of Congress Cataloging-in-Publication Data
Moon, Janell
        The Mouth of Home First Edition

ISBN 0-9657015-2-2
Moon, Janell—Poetry 2. Women authors, United States—20th century—Poetry. 3. Lesbians—United States—Poetry. 4. Aging—United States—Poetry. 5. Family—United States—Poetry.

Library of Congress Catalog Card Number: 98-74910

Acknowledgments

Selections from this book, some in earlier versions, have appeared in the following periodicals: *The Writer's Voice, New Collage Magazine, Amethyst, The Red Rock Review*, and *The National Forum*.

With heartfelt thanks to CB Follett, Lonnie Hull Dupont, Dorothy Wall, Phyllis Burke, Diane di Prima for listening and/or helping me put this volume into form. To the members of San Francisco's *Sunday Child Art Salon*, for their encouragement. To Bonnie Marzlak, and Claire Wolf Kranz, for their love and belief in me. To my son, Greg, for his kindness and gentle ways, and to Eileen, Emert, Douglas, and Judy, my original family who valued creativity in all forms. And to Ohio, whose rivers, fields, and trees gave me my first dreaming places.

The poems may have happened, were likely to happen, could have happened, almost happened, felt like they happened, or should have happened. Even fiction is true.

Contents

III. *Fortune Telling*

To Suzanne, always

LIFE MODEL

Travels

Rain on the child's cheek,
continued baptism,
as he passes through
scratchy fields and tumbled hills.
Here he is enjoying his new
yellow umbrella and he strips
naked and paddles the gutters
to the ocean's mouth. Before
he knows it, he is swept to the island
of strangers who lead him to
a table of fruit and fish.
When he looks towards his feet,
he sees he is no longer a boy.
Open drawers hold new longings
and new appetites. A woman
standing nearby holds three choices:
finish the chapter, start a new story,
sit down at the table and eat.

No Word For Marigold

They didn't have marigolds in Poland
and besides my mama and papa emigrated
before they learned the names of flowers,
so many words buried and born under the foot of change,
the blue roofs of Poland gone.
On the boat, Mama's sister lost to fever,
Grandma's fingers sliding over rosary beads
as the boat crashed through the rocking waters
to New York, war bonds taped to their chests,
their name changed with the humid temperature.
On to the mines of Pennsylvania,
a steady paycheck, the toil of mules.
Grandma sewed labels in furs
for ladies in cities, her small stitches hardly seen.
How would you write your life as story?
How would I? If you remember
the place that first held your cry,
would it shape your life?
My parents yearned to be close to the land
of their birth, had to decide between the smells
of history and carrots and meat.
I spent the first half of my life listening
to what they didn't know and what they had to do.
Mama showed me how to make kielbasa
as Papa studied for his citizen papers.
On hot nights, he'd read to us, no sleep
until the neighbors quieted
and the air cooled down. From the high shelf,
he'd get the family's treasured
story book, legends of children disappearing
in the sweeping snows of winter,
the woods behind the house, how they were lost then found.
We'd ask to hear again the part where the village
men struggled through any weather, any danger

to save children from wolves, from nature's hand,
plenty of mashed potato soup to nourish them
at the end of their scare. After we tried
his patience and knew we wouldn't get one more story,
one more reading, we could sometimes talk him into tracing
with his finger our picture book, our eager minds memorizing:
lily, blue jay, eucalyptus.

Why We Are Born

Curses hang on tiny strings from the rafters
of my disheveled childhood. My father
reads his books and doesn't notice.
I light a black candle to show the messages
of warning, shouts
from the white-white parchment
as danger swings back and forth, back and forth.
I am alone with what I know.

I wrap the candle in the paper, fling it
down the country road.
Let hatred burn to the ground. I live

each day crossing the river to my life.

Life Model

When death comes to tap my seat
on the ferris wheel, reminding me
there are others waiting
and I have paid enough,
leave my face showing age
and love and disappointment.

I hear sounds of shuffling people.
The model, robed for the moment.
Then a hush as a human steps up
to the platform
to show her nakedness.

Inheritance

She staggers under the weight
of suitcases, hat boxes with photographs,
Grandfather's old clock, the one she learned
to tell time on. Up there on the hill
over the Mississippi, she could let
the day slip by watching steamers,
could lie on her back in the tomato
patch with a shaker of salt, spend early evenings
at the cemetery hopscotching on the graves
of her family. Each winter the rain
would slide more of them into the hillside.
She liked the idea of their bones getting
mixed up, her gay great uncle, her stern
auntie, the traveling cousin who married
the tightrope walker, the dancers
who left behind pink netting
and chiffon, the auntie who painted
the shine of sun
on the families' almond eyes.
She wanted to lie in the dirt
with them on those summer nights,
dance with their stories, play
with their ghosts. She wanted them to know
she wrote stories of the sweet taffy and bitter
knots of their lives.

Dealing with Grandma

After Grandpa died, Grandma moved to the beach
and grew to hate the sound of the ocean,
those waves washing day and night.
She moved to Texas and hated
the bugs but liked the accent.
"Quaint," she called it. She liked
the wider streets of Kansas City
and the poetry readings of Ann Arbor,
That's what the living do sometimes,"
my mother said, "they wander."
My grandma's Chicago canopy
over the entrance of her apartment
changed colors with every move,
the Murphy bed, the radiator in different
corners. Up against the window
in her new place, a willow tree
but no refrigerator. She bought
a wire basket and hung it outside the window, a place
to cool alligator pears and brown eggs
on a fall night. She wanted no one with her.
She'd tell you to your face, "Go home."
When summer's heat became a problem
she moved to Hyde Park,
a place of cheap housing for university students.
She liked it there among the youngsters trying to find
their soul's code.

Ohio Childhood

Stay! I wanted to stay!
Pearl Street, Barwell, Wyandotte Avenue,
apples in the trees, train flares
tucked in woolen pockets, trains passing
through the valley on the way to Omaha.
I never wanted to move from my window
seat in winter, the sound of the furnace, the smell
of burning coal, my bed next to the heater
warming my feet in the mornings, my fingers
making dragons on the frosted window.
In summer, lilies-of-the-valley and the smell
of garden corn and tomatoes, the sounds
of the children playing games in the street,
hop-scotch and kick-the-can. When it was
79 degrees we were allowed to ask my mother
to take us swimming and sometimes she
drove both ways, my young body slicing
water like a knife through custard. I could
do anything then: outrun the fastest boy,
sing off-key and not care. Heaven
drifted through my braided hair. I never wanted
to leave the sun coming up over the maples,
the prattling of jays reproaching the robins.

The Yardstick

I've lived in San Francisco
so long and from the first moment
loved the gingerbread houses on the hillsides,
the angles of roofs making stairstep
patterns, the parakeets in the palm trees. Houses
with small yards of pampas grass, bamboo, bottle brush.

But now visiting these wide stretches of street
in my childhood's Ohio, I see the green wings
of trees, the sweep of lawns and remember gathering
grasses in the stretch of my sweater,
realize I have carried green in my arms
all my life. And look at this! Open space,
flat land, devil strips near the street to roll on.
I am lost in memory of the ice man, the rag man
calling through the changing seasons.

Good Luck

Margaret Eggleston said she was lucky
because she had such an American name.
She thought this gave her an advantage
in contests, her days
filled with entry forms, writing
jingles, essays on the benefits
of sturdy shoes for walking
or corn flakes for breakfast. She could
rhyme any word and in one paragraph
sweep you across the plains
of city or country life.

We kids peeked at her as she went from door
to door collecting magazines from housewives
wiping their countertops clean. By midday,
she'd appear with a pile of stamped envelopes
for the corner mailbox.

The best day was when a van delivered to her
the first television of the neighborhood. Once
it was a waffle iron, another time garbage cans
made out of ruffled plastic not tin.

We'd determine to spend our summer days clipping,
filling, mailing contest coupons, hoping for a convertible
for our dad, a set of hand-painted china
in bold colors for our mom
but the sun would draw us to the quarry, the cool
of evening to sidewalks smooth
for skating, the dark to look for new worlds
through the telescope out back.

My Mother Was a Lady

My father was easy to trick, a university man
taken to daydreaming. You could turn off the hose
and he'd continue to hold it aimed toward grass.
He'd go down to the basement to fetch my mother's
ironing basket and come back with a stack
of old Life magazines.
He left kitchen cupboards open, the drawers ajar,
once our neighbor thought there had been a robbery–
everything thrown open and spilling.

My mother set up a tool bench
so he could repair things
but he didn't have any nails.
For ten years the door to the television room
leaned against the cement wall
in the basement waiting to be painted
until my mother threw it out.
I remember the day my father tried
to change the toilet seat, the paint scraped
through the years by women's rings
as they wiped themselves, my mother said.
He unbolted the seat and couldn't
get the new one on, company coming
in an hour. My mother became unhinged
but never mentioned a word to the company
leaving the women to hold themselves up
over the toilet to save themselves.

Dreams

Mirrors hold reflections of past summer nights,
small towns with narrow streets,
the barker's call from the carnival
at the edge of town. Neon-lit roller coasters,
children tumbling and falling
with screams of excitement,
as a woman sits in her bedroom
brushing her hair. With each brushstroke
the twilight deepens, the moon climbs
the ladder to the sky; how far, the rings
of Saturn, the skin of Jupiter and Mars.
She dresses in satin and silver gloves,
walks to the turning of the Ferris wheel,
so high she might
catch what she wants.

Imprints of the Mind

They found her in a Russian orphanage
sitting straight and tall on a small wooden chair
while her teacher took her photograph.
If she were good, her mother
would come back for her. Well, my
friends came back the next year
with papers that said she could go
with them to California
to be their little girl.
She clung to her new mothers
before she went to sleep at night.
The feeling that once made her sit
in that little chair
seemed to have turned to prancing.
In her dreams she could see shadows
of her Russian mother and she wasn't sure
if she should sit down.

New Lands

My brother spent his childhood digging,
our backyard looking like a
human gopher patch. Sometimes you could see
only the cowlick of the crown of his head
as he sat in his hole, the shovel flinging Ohio dirt.
I wondered what he was looking for:
his mind, his body. Sometimes, he'd put grasses
and sticks over the top to make a trap but we
were into survival and knew not to go out back
in the dark. This was before any talk of land mines
or schizophrenia. Maybe he was digging his way
to China. I was in the attic, dreaming
with colored crayons, making up words to add
to the dictionary.

Collecting

My aunt, a golden-haired actress,
used the sleeve of her sweater
to hold tissues to wipe her tears
as she'd tell me stories. Some I'd heard
before in milder versions from my mother;
her retelling seemed quite different.
My favorite was when she blurted out secrets
about the men she loved while she traveled,
the one with the boots he never took off,
the other with a love of lace.
When I'd ask her, she'd tell me, "Texas,"
describing a convertible ride
across the flat country
into the mossy nights of Mississippi.
"And jail," I asked, "when were you in jail?"
She'd cry and tell stories of youth's betrayals
and deep cuts in the earth.
I'd beg her to start at the beginning, slowly
turn the page, but I was the orderly writer and she,
in the spotlight, acted out what came
across her stage.

Born Into

I was born into a family of heterosexuals.
No matter how the merry-go-round turned,
it is the fact that circled my life. My brother
who had canaries enter his mind at 19 years,
still had a girlfriend. Even my sister who
imagined herself a victim of polio and various
poisons married an easy-going plumber.
There I was in my plaid skirts and bobby socks
following the tomboy down the street to
her softball games and I didn't know why.
Show me a girl who was angry and I'd bake her cookies.
Let a girl's collar get mussed and I'd fix it.
If a girl let me cut her hair, I was captured.

I didn't want to marry but my mother said
no woman did.
Now I'm single and I wonder
what that tomboy is doing—maybe a black belt
competing in the Gay Olympics, an employee of Nike.
Me? I moved to California, go out Saturday
nights with a special woman on my arm.

CRY AND RESPONSE

After All These Years

My college roommate found my poems
in an anthology she was reading
and wrote to me after
twenty-five years. Ten days later, my other roommate
wrote, the trio complete. Not that we sang
together. Dating, learning the twist,
recklessly diving off rocks above the stone quarry,
curling our eyelashes made us close.
One married during her last year of college
and soon after, her husband hit her.
The other criticized my fiancé
because she would marry for money.
My husband, who swept the kitchen
and ran my bath, was a good man
but I was unhappy.
I guess they circled back looking for the laughter
they remembered.
When I wrote them about Sarah,
they never wrote again.
It made me quiet for awhile
but with her help I turned my attention
to living the life I loved.

Sweets

A man speaks to me
his eyes wandering over my sweater
following the buttons to my breasts
a certain lift in his voice
his wife hasn't heard in years

I give his wife my smile
linger my attention over her meal
ask her does she want more cream
perhaps a touch of honey

Shadows

I am afraid of what
she is afraid of

she warns me she'll want sex
schedule it to suit her
make me cook for her
the way she likes it
take the fish and throw it back
storm around
make rain

guess she hasn't smelled
the swamp mud on me
lightning in my fingertips
thunder in my chest
puddle splasher
people eater
serve up broken glass

she tells me she's difficult
I think witches, flying bats
good match.

Mother's Grave

Mother, you are hovering above the plot
of your life but you are alive.
Didn't you once speed
beyond state lines
in a yellow Thunderbird
to Arizona, then flee
toward Texas because you liked hot weather
and large bodies of water? Remember,
teaching me to swim the Rio Grande?
You took the pony
to the creek and let your red hair fly.
I want to watch your life
come to an end with the flashes of delight
of your own stories: roping fear,
committing gluttony, riding desire.

No Maturing Perhaps

I hate sharing food and the people in my life
know this. I sometimes see them exchanging
glances and laughing, one wearing my sock, the other
with $20.00 of mine in her pocket. Once a woman
broke up with me when I wouldn't share my cashew
chicken, her mother and her eating tofu broccoli and
tofu mushroom. Since it came to that, I thought, it
was for the best, the mother carrying her own bell
to ring for extra service. Now I'm at the beach with my nephew
eating my personal-sized pizza. I see him lift his head
to see what I'm eating but he doesn't ask if those are
anchovies. This, the reason I vacation with him.

Making a Whole

How might my pen describe the color
of the Atlantic Ocean in a way
that would help you be with me?
Some mention of shimmering light,
a navy blue world?
I could take a photograph
that would show humid air,
heat and moisture entering my skin
letting it soften and relax.
The smell of salt breeze springs
between grasses,
the sound of surf frightening
before a coming storm.
You would see a simple moon over water,
quiet time to dream and ponder.
It's like lying in your arms,
lovemaking over, trying to describe what makes
our time together special. We've had relationships
where desire would fling itself out
to fields of horses and ride.
This time it paws the dirt and stays.
Perhaps we could paint to show love's pant,
let music raise the tide of heart.

Once Marked

I have been spooning the river
for many years now
and I have found many things:
the silver of my mother, the
coin of my father's family,
gold smuggled to Switzerland.
Nazi gold, they call it, stolen
from the Jews and
from us, the first ones taken
to the camps, pink triangles
sewn on our sleeves.
My mother told me she once
watched a village of women
paraded down her narrow street
branded with the shape of a triangle
on their shoulders,
the burns still blistering,
their eyes bullets.
We know what it's like to be haunted.
Just to read of a woman stalked
makes the tiny hairs on my neck tingle.
Pray in a strange church and the air
may become heavy as the prison
it once was even though it's now spring.
We'll sense it every time.
Sit next to an uncle
who seems pleasant enough and the smell
of something rotten will make us search
for tissues and exits. So many times
I count my week's wages to see if I am safe.
So many times I make lists of friends.
Sisters on the piles of dead, our sisters
on the piles of dead. I want my body to forget,
to notice the sky, the clearest blue
I've ever seen.

Loss. It Starts As We Begin

How could I know when I left
Ohio's winding roads
for California's poppies,
I'd spend most of my life alone.
I was young and foolish, following
radio dreams and surf, wanting poetry,
licorice nights, warm hands of women.
Friends, I added one a year
until there was a circle
that in time dwindled
as marriage, another baby
claimed their time. Some thought I talked too
much, another was afraid of my sex.
Clouds came and moved on by.
I lived the crystal day.

Trying Something New

I look for a new source for poetry,
take Muni downtown:
perhaps record some interesting dialogue,
a crazy outfit or two.
The minute the door closes
I remember why I don't ride Muni.
I can't breath.
You'd think because I'm a hypnotist,
I'd be over this.
I remember that nice young woman
who used to sweat so badly from fear,
she couldn't hold on
to the overhead rail.
One rainy night,
the train got stuck in an underground
tunnel and she stayed cool as ice.
Even when she got to my office
30 minutes late, she was
cool. I'm always glad to see success.

So here I am wanting
to put my mouth
to an open window but these new trains
have air conditioning.
The train makes a whirling sound.
I get off feeling dizzy and have milk.
The financial district—I didn't know they had sun
down here. Crowds make me crazy.
I walk home, each block easing
my breath. I like to write
with the front door open.

Harmony

A lovely day to take a beach walk
with a friend. I tell her when I learned
cement wasn't earth. She responds with
the day she first learned books were written
by people. Turning points
in our lives: mine, the world changed
by men and machines.
Hers, a world of possibility.
We sit on the boulders
the construction crew piled high
at the end of the beach
to protect the summer homes,
write poems,
her energy drawing me
to the smell of paper and binding paste
when I worked
in the high-ceilinged one-room library
trying to hush my giggle of youth.
The sun-speckled bay touches the tabby sand
in front of us as the steamers pass by
on their way to China.

Sometimes Good Comes

I lived protected by a husband
who wanted my body,
a body that couldn't love him.
Oh, it wasn't that I didn't get pregnant:
stillborns, a miscarriage, blood
running down my leg to the nurse's pan.
Always the feeling of capture.
How fettered our talk became
never mentioning desire or disaster.
Finally a living thing
was wrung from the ice
of my body,
the birth coming fast.
One moment I was falling,
pain loosening my grip on the stretcher
and then as I fell
a breath to love
tumbled out of my body.

The World As It Is

We sit in a round tent as Billy Graham prays his gospel. He's saying homosexuality is a sin but Christians shouldn't pick on us. There are so many sins, even good Christians may sin sometimes. I tell my friend we shouldn't be here.

I introduce my son's girlfriend to my boss and he says he thought she was mine. She laughs, says her father would call me "that lesbian, the one who likes girls," but he'd shake my hand. Her stepmother would act nice but keep her gloved hands in her pockets. My ex-husband says our son's low self-esteem is because of my weird lifestyle. His new wife says that she doesn't believe in lesbians.

"Leprechauns?" I ask, thinking I heard wrong.

"No," my son replies, "She doesn't believe I have a mother."

Drama

A crash on the ragged rocks
of the Cliff House
and you'll be on Channel 5.
Here in San Francisco,
we've all talked about
the flight to the rocks
and a final loneliness,
a heroine dying for love,
ravens flapping their licorice wings,
foghorns mourning–
a hero eating his last meal
before the jump.
In my caution,
on dreary days, I keep a distance
from those rugged shores,
get in bed to watch
the 10 o'clock news, then spend the night
thrashing about dreaming of military tanks,
that dog caught up
in a rush of flood water in Missouri.

The Burning

It was a night when strangers talked.
Perhaps it was the flames
shooting destruction nearby
that jarred our tongues.
Whatever was strung, chatter broke around me
caressed in grace. This time, grace.
Finally everyone disappeared behind closed doors.
I could smell charred wood, meatloaf and green beans.
Adults danced to the radio,
children were read a book that night.
When sleep came, there was no yearning for dawn.
No cry for the changing sky. We were happy
to sleep, pillows touching.

When morning broke, there was a moment
when light and dark shone in balance
and if we really focused,
we could see what was left,
what was worthy.

The Brave

It was hot that summer day,
the streets outside Barcelona
crammed with villagers and visitors
waiting to run the streets with the bulls.
This was the run of the commoner,
no matador's fancy capework
or muleta needed to entice the bull
into charging, Only courage needed,
just like when a woman
in love murmurs,
"Anything. I will do anything."

Moving on

If I were a big person with an understanding heart,
I'd take what my friends offered me with thanks.
Ask my spirit to hold me tighter. Help me sleep
deeper. Bring new dreams to light.

But I'm small and I don't feel as if I have any
real friends. Just people who want to go to movies.
The week my partner and I break up, they
ask how I am doing? Listen several minutes
then turn the conversation to hiking boots. A new
book they've read. A favorite restaurant I should
try. Then it's how are my other friends.

The next week it's, do you have that flu that's
going around? Oh, you mean your feelings.
I try to hurry down the healing road but I'm
broken. My chest's been kicked and I
have no one to lift the shoe.

I'm too needy to lose anyone else so I pretend
I'm okay. But I number times they listen to me,
limit future favors.

Virginia

Those stones in your pockets,
the rushing water
make danger live in our hand.
You make it an option
and it scares me to be so close.
You don't mind we unseed your letters,
husk out the truth. You left
it to us. But there are so many truths,
the river, the river bank, the turn
of your body, the current. How can
we know what is best.
There was a chill in the air that night
and I could hear crackling
through the trees, water hitting
rocks and you. The world moves fast
outside the flowered curtains.
Were there rings of fire on your wrists?
Did you ever write a poem in the shape of night?

Freedom

I am saving or losing my life
swimming exhaustedly in one direction,
no sense of land.
What matters is breath, in and out,
in and out,
my strong arms,
the sound of lapping.
Have you
ever been in a world filled with just
your sound? A time when
the world held your body
in a quiet
while you stormed.

Love and Death and Deep Cuts in the Earth

I wouldn't have eaten your body. Even though
I circled you those last days as the cuts
in the earth widened between us. I would
have left you your body. I was on the chain
fastened to the steel stake, my life swinging
around, repeating itself, repeating itself.
Now I wish like the raven I had flown
to the cliffs, taken my eggs and tucked
them in the soft sand of the harbor.
Oh, I was so cold! And though I imagined
your harming—a knife, a gun, scissors—
eaten you, no! I'm an egalitarian,
humanitarian, vegetarian.

The Homeless

She holds an empty bag
and the body of a Gibson guitar,
head and strings gone.
She carries it like a precious thing,
like a harp played at a graveside,
like a harmonica held in the thick
hands of the blind man
pilgrimaging towards food.
Not dead yet, she drinks from cups
left on the round tables in the café,
squirts half and half into a water glass.
What's next, I wonder
handing her five dollars.

Cry and Response

The bird flew from the sky's blue blanket
into the church's sanctuary.
Fluttering at the wall; it couldn't stop;
its flapping wings heard
over the congregation's prayer.
The priest swung his rod and incense,
asked for holy presence,
a quiet in His house. Then he called,
"Why have you come, why have you come?"

The bird cawed back, "Why ask me? I'm in your hands."

FORTUNE TELLING

Fortune Telling

The obvious is not the truth. Oh, I see
your swinging crystal earrings, your dress
of the bluest-blue, and these are lovely.
But fashion is not the true nature of your life
or how you have been colored. There was a lifting
of shaded eyes somewhere in your sixteenth
year, the summer you took
a speedboat to the caves behind the waterfall
where life was moist. Remember it was then
you first saw life in the dark?

Now you're holding and flying, holding and flying.
Look at the trapeze that swings
to meet your hand, the net removed, see
the falling of your body. You must turn to those
who once loved you. They've been answering
since you've been gone.

You want to know more of what lies ahead.
Your hands stained with the ink of the stories
you write, bourbon and wire. Your feet can't travel
one more dog's length to soft fur and silk.
I can tell you of a sand painting beneath your feet,
the sun-baked sand holding
the steady steps of the camel, a ladder strung
across the lit miles. The desert will open
to your buttered desires once you start
this journey. The ruby cactus forecasts your future
by its blossoming. It is this oasis that offers
the water you're seeking.

The View

The radio
man drones on and on.
I can't listen
did he say ride our butts
now the rain now the rain
even though I saw the sun.
Silence with a dread of
emergency. Hang up the phone. That sound will go
on and on. Take care of daily things.

How can you listen and not hang up?
The sound of day
inside the house. To be caged. Water
doesn't sound much different from
a gun. All the wars I've been spared and
I'm not spared at all. Everyone I love is tying
dark pockets of fear. The sky is full
of dreams and the sound of planes,
Blue Angels somersaulting.
How these Angels waste my money.
The bass drums on.
women walk the block and stare.
Tell me what I know.
This is no place. The world spins.
Like any good woman,
I kick through the tulips,
plant my shoes at the mouth of home.

No Picture

There's a plane streaking across the sky,
it looks like the pathway to God.
My ex is married to a woman
who gambles. My son says I can always come live
with him but he hasn't moved out yet.
He made the same offer to his dad.
Who knew? A leaf hangs caught in a cobweb
high outside my window. Growth,
first a mass of green. Now harbored in autumn
before the swipe of my broom.
The winds come and blow the chimes
hanging from my avocado tree
and each day I climb the rocky
side of the beach before turning back
to the long stretch of sand
unribboning itself to the stripe of ocean,
the spread of the sky's design. I'd been fingering
through a notion box searching for a match
to a lost button, a thread that might come close enough.
Mending and walking the shore relaxes me,
watching the gulls give warning before taking
the orange from the hand of a child who
knowing he can't catch them
feels brave enough to chase them.
Oh, this push and pull.
Love doesn't seem to know
if it wants a saddled horse or a wild ride. In San Pablos
the burros stand on sidewalks with flowers
behind their ears while the young
men flash their teeth and their camera,
"Picture, señora?" but I won't do that to the burro.

Last Time

The last thing I did when I was young
was to go to Rio with my Cuban lover.
We were unplanned and reckless.
Jesus held out his arms for us
from the highest hill, the train ride up
making us feel cross in the heat.
After fevered prayers at his feet, we went
back to the beach, happy it had
no biting flies, buying beer and bracelets
from women walking the sand
holding these treasures in their blankets.
We returned to our room to make love and nap
before putting on our Saturday night best
and getting our nerve up to ask a taxi driver
if there were any gay bars. He looked surprised
and drove us to a club where a woman
did sexual acts with a large snake.

Now my world has turned into days of wrinkles and worry
with only lavender and lilac softening
the edges of age and neck pain.
I went to a party for a neighbor last night
and the young women were wearing black
lace slips, each taking turns
dancing in the birthday gown,
a floor-length taffeta net.
They insisted I take a turn and I was happy
to dance in a formal one more time,
could even zip it all the way up!
The youngsters smoked cigarettes
and I remembered the feeling
of wildness when I smoked,
the glow of tiny red lights swaying through the room.

Crow's Feet

If laugh lines were adolescent,
I'd be young again.
Instead I'm munching on secrets,
sitting under the family lamp that knows
the whole story but can't talk.
I remember when I fashioned
through the room
in my wrinkled prom gown,
the only girl in my class wearing emerald green
not pastel. How excited I was to stay up past midnight.
Now go to work
in tie shoes, occasionally buckled shoes,
step around wet grasses
and edges that sharply drop.
My friend says it's not because
we're afraid of falling
but afraid of jumping.
I search the house for my keys and jacket,
nod when talking to my neighbors
wishing I could remember their names
after knowing them for twenty years
and forget about the promise of dinner with you
at our favorite restaurant
while I make ham for dinner.
I'm sweeping my screened-in porch
over and over. I'd sing if something could
start me. I prune the evergreens in triangles,
the maples let to go wild.

The Holy Grail

We wrote questions of the holy grail, the why
are we here, why are we here, as the little
boat on the ocean bobbed in the night breeze.
We asked why of everything that summer,
wanted the world to be thrown to our feet
in answers. When the world grew tired
of our questioning, she moved her warmth
toward the south country
leaving us with winter's breath,
time to gather wood for the fire.

Love Poem

It's late afternoon and raining.
Love is on my mind and tide pools, red lava,
and wrinkled skin. What's left for love, I wonder?
I have licked sores for many years now,
tasted my own blood. I've put a flower at the altar
for each poem I've written, for each life I've not lived.
I like the flowering eucalyptus, how every part of its
life cycle shows at the same time, the seed and bloom,
the bud. It creates a life and lives it.
Maybe life is like a poem, live and let it find you.
Watching you sleep, I lose things, let go.
I don't know how to help what went wrong with myself.
And, there are many things I'm never going to do.
The dried roses on the shelf,
the lilies thrown across time ask me
to let the circus come, bring spring to
the trees again.

At a Poetry Reading, Oh Art!

I was at the café and the kids
were all there with their wild-fashioned hair
and facial tattoos. Earlier I had a slice of pizza
next door in a place where a customer and
clerk were silently fighting over the opened/shut
door. I stayed at my corner seat, my stomach
tight about fighting. Mostly I know about losing.
When I went out, I asked some guys
not to sit on my car, luckily the bus
came and they all got up.

I was thinking of the night we met,
how shiny your hair was falling
out of your braid. I wanted to feel
your cherry-nippled breast
against my back as I dreamt
the warm night through,
wanted to put a candle in my cap
like Van Gogh did
so he could paint the stars,
see love with a different face
and there you were telling me it didn't
take poetry or death to reach a star.

Heating the Towels After Her Bath

I'm afraid I'll fall in love and polish her shoes,
spend the night crowded on a inch of the bed,
sleeping in a room with the bay trees shuttered from sight,
so she can be sheltered in just the right way.
I'm afraid I'll turn off the television before the news
I like to watch, stay on the same page of my
meditation book for a month, wear silk,
my shoulders cold all night.

I know it's a bad habit but I like to brush my teeth
then have a diet cola (Pepsi, the underdog),
light natural popcorn, fall asleep with the television on
and the light flaming. I like waking for an hour in
the middle of the night continuing my evening
with no one scolding me. Of course, this way
no one's holding me either.

I loved the mother that fed me pineapple but I've had
trouble in relationships with women.
When a woman says, "Don't talk, not a whisper,"
I don't wonder why
as I might with a man,
I just begin to think how I could live as a post card:
canceled stamp, postmark,
message and address, the signature of my lover coming first.

Getting Old's Not So Bad

I make a list and soon want to follow my penciled goals to attend poetry readings, bathe in mineral waters, walk under the flowering elms in the park. Perhaps I'll send my son to scout the better readers, find the warmer days, determine the day before the first bloom. I'm a pedestrian now, no longer drive a car. I carry various diagnoses instead of a briefcase. Get to wear low shoes and have a nap and dream away the places I'll never have to go.

Dawn

The sky lightens and I live
the life I've always wanted.
I need no hummingbirds whirring
near my window seeking nectar,
no primroses placed to the west for luck
or strings of shining lights
lining the boulevards. I shake
the apple tree outside my window,
ask God to come down, stay close to me.

Language, Words and Poetry

The mind must organize. These are not
ears of pears, that boy is not a polished son,
keys hanging in a row, similar
not mattering
which. You wouldn't weave a turkey although
you might skip a stone. Some would even speak
to their toes to find out the cause of pain.
The woods are vast, we are but
a minute from the depth
of the thicket, mud's jelly
releasing sulfur. It's a scream of dislike;
it could be a scream of pleasure
or of contentment sitting on the blue-webbed chair.
Lavender spills and heals the knee,
a nest fills with pearls round as potatoes.
It's more than poetry's imagination that whispers
on a harsh night.

Little Bits of String

A cartoon shows two cats talking to each other, one saying that people are okay but he prefers tiny bits of string. I agree as I watch my friend prune her bushes to a mere stick jutting out of the ground, her flowers pulled before any necessary weeding. It reminds me of the man next door who owns a two flat, won't rent it because people are messy. And here I sit at the foot of this table with the hostess's formal silver piled in front of me: silverware, goblets, large candelabras. Guest talk around the mounds. Once I thought if I talked gaily to even the most troubled souls, I would be saved. Now I know that the world doesn't follow order. Green waits for the rain and sometimes the rains don't come. Take the silver: wrap it in your napkin, just in case.

The Personal Is Political

If you want to write a universal poem, think of
something you care enough about that might raise
the story to the field of humanity.   —A man

As a woman, I have lived giving from the drained well of my body, never asking for pure water. I married to please everyone but myself, no pictures in the movies of decent women loving another woman, flowers in her hair. I didn't even know what was missing since no magazine entered our house that showed diversity or love's winding road. I sat and ate the food on my plate that Mother made for me, gave Father money from my baby sitting to save for college. It took many years of education before my dead body rose.

Blessing

Once I only saw your wonders.
Now I know you and all your inexcusable ways.
Don't be cross with me, I didn't write them down.
I won't say them in public.
I know you chose me
because I reminded you of your favorite aunt,
who washed your hair each morning, dried
it in a thick blue towel. But did you know
that once I kissed the earth of your head,
I could no longer ride the hard hill
on my miserable horse?

A Woman's Life

As I get older, my bosom gets larger.
I meditate and think of apples.
Try to clear my mind but get more apples.
I breathe in the mountain, out the meadow.
Try for some relaxation.
Not to worry about money.
Not to worry about my palpitating heart.
Just sit there in my women's circle,
try to get a grip.

I'm glad the weekend's about over.
I'm exhausted. Went on a trip to the river
with an old friend. She never stops.
I usually drag along okay but this time
I was far behind.
I like to be with people but don't like chatter.
When I do talk, I like understanding. Right away.
I told her I was having troubles at the office.
She said I had trouble at my last job.
As if I need reminding. I don't think at my age
it's easy to make friends. Or be with people.

I go home and straighten the kitchen.
Enjoy my oranges and cranberries.
Check the fridge: what's
for dinner. Remember my sick friend.
Make a note to make an appointment for
a check up. Write a poem
about getting older. Put on
comfortable shoes. Take a walk.
Think this is the best time of life right now.
So much happiness in bubble baths and teas.
Or reading. I like to read stories of women
with happy endings. Living and then dying.
Going to seed.

A Million More

after Judy Grahn

For every one of us
there is a million more
and for those million
another million.
Every time you love,
a million more
who love like you.
A million
women understand,
a million men.
Even as you think
you are alone,
a million more
understand yearning,
hear your calling.
There is a voice
that says what you say
a million times,
a voice that calls
to the page written
around the world:
the ginger pickers in the field,
the Caribbean shell snatchers.
You can love who you love.
You are a part of these ways,
these humans, millions, these millions.
Listen.

Wise Blood

Before childhood existed, there was Medusa,
her gaze able to
turn men into stone. She left no ivory
comb on any man's dresser,
wore a steel and ruby ring
on her wedding finger given to herself
the night of her first menstruation.
Her eyes shone the silver feminine.
Her serpent head asked for justice and equality,
asking women to eat the pomegranate,
eat the pomegranate
not the apple, saying,
"I am all that has been, is, will be."

Contentment

It isn't always April, those days
when gold rings the trees,
wraps the night in silk.
How different from the dry days of August
when the grass mowed and watered, still yellows.
Hay covering meadows raked in rectangles
setting a geometry for horses soon needing
winter's rest.

In the dark moist days
after the animals are fed, I sleep too.
In my youth, I was seldom idle, now I welcome
my hands on my lap dreaming near you.
I remember nimble fingers, chords on your back,
tunes that live on in the eaves of our house;
the boards on the floor cut in spring.